A Boy's Road
of
Memories!

A Boy's Travel Journal

Activinotes

Activinotes

DAILY JOURNALS, PLANNERS, NOTEBOOKS AND OTHER BLANK BOOKS

Place to explore : _____   Date _____

One Moment I want to Remember :

_____
_____
_____
_____
_____
_____
_____
_____

Doodle here

Quick list of stuff I've done here :

_____
_____
_____
_____
_____
_____
_____

One major way this place is different from home :

_____
_____
_____
_____

One major way this place is the same as ome :

_____
_____
_____
_____

Place to explore : _____   Date _____

One Moment I want to Remember :
_____
_____
_____
_____
_____
_____
_____
_____

Doodle here

Quick list of stuff I've done here :
_____
_____
_____
_____
_____
_____
_____

One major way this place is different from home :

_____
_____
_____
_____

One major way this place is the same as ome :

_____
_____
_____
_____

Place to explore : _____   Date _____

One Moment I want to Remember :

_____
_____
_____
_____
_____
_____
_____
_____
_____

Doodle here

Quick list of stuff I've done here :

_____
_____
_____
_____
_____
_____
_____

One major way this place is different from home :

_____
_____
_____
_____

One major way this place is the same as ome :

_____
_____
_____
_____

Place to explore : _____   Date _____

One Moment I want to Remember :

_____
_____
_____
_____
_____
_____
_____
_____

Doodle here

Quick list of stuff I've done here :

_____
_____
_____
_____
_____
_____
_____

One major way this place is different from home :

_____
_____
_____
_____

One major way this place is the same as ome :

_____
_____
_____
_____

Place to explore : _____ Date _____

One Moment I want to Remember :

_____
_____
_____
_____
_____
_____
_____
_____

Doodle here

Quick list of stuff I've done here :

_____
_____
_____
_____
_____
_____
_____

One major way this place is different from home :

_____
_____
_____
_____

One major way this place is the same as ome :

_____
_____
_____
_____

Place to explore : _____   Date _____

One Moment I want to Remember :

_____

_____

_____

_____

_____

_____

_____

_____

Doodle here

Quick list of stuff I've done here :

_____

_____

_____

_____

_____

_____

_____

One major way this place is different from home :

_____

_____

_____

_____

One major way this place is the same as ome :

_____

_____

_____

_____

Place to explore : _____ Date _____

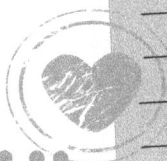

One Moment I want to Remember :

_____
_____
_____
_____
_____
_____
_____
_____
_____

Doodle here

Quick list of stuff I've done here :

_____
_____
_____
_____
_____
_____
_____

One major way this place is different from home :

_____
_____
_____
_____

One major way this place is the same as ome :

_____
_____
_____
_____

Place to explore : _____   Date _____

One Moment I want to Remember :
_____
_____
_____
_____
_____
_____
_____
_____

Doodle here

Quick list of stuff I've done here :
_____
_____
_____
_____
_____
_____
_____

One major way this place is different from home :

_____
_____
_____
_____

One major way this place is the same as ome :

_____
_____
_____
_____

Place to explore : _____   Date _____

One Moment I want to Remember :
_____
_____
_____
_____
_____
_____
_____
_____

Doodle here

Quick list of stuff I've done here :
_____
_____
_____
_____
_____
_____
_____

One major way this place is different from home :

_____
_____
_____
_____

One major way this place is the same as ome :

_____
_____
_____
_____

Place to explore : _____   Date _____

One Moment I want to Remember :

_____
_____
_____
_____
_____
_____
_____
_____
_____

Doodle here

Quick list of stuff I've done here :

_____
_____
_____
_____
_____
_____
_____

One major way this place is different from home :

_____
_____
_____
_____

One major way this place is the same as ome :

_____
_____
_____
_____

Place to explore : _____   Date _____

One Moment I want to Remember :

_____
_____
_____
_____
_____
_____
_____
_____
_____

Doodle here

Quick list of stuff I've done here :

_____
_____
_____
_____
_____
_____
_____

One major way this place is different from home :

_____
_____
_____
_____

One major way this place is the same as ome :

_____
_____
_____
_____

Place to explore : _____   Date _____

One Moment I want to Remember :
_____
_____
_____
_____
_____
_____
_____
_____
_____

Doodle here

Quick list of stuff I've done here :
_____
_____
_____
_____
_____
_____
_____

One major way this place is different from home :

_____
_____
_____
_____

One major way this place is the same as ome :

_____
_____
_____
_____

Place to explore : _____   Date _____

One Moment I want to Remember :

_____
_____
_____
_____
_____
_____
_____
_____
_____

Doodle here

Quick list of stuff I've done here :

_____
_____
_____
_____
_____
_____
_____

One major way this place is different from home :

_____
_____
_____
_____

One major way this place is the same as ome :

_____
_____
_____
_____

Place to explore : _____   Date _____

One Moment I want to Remember :

_____
_____
_____
_____
_____
_____
_____
_____
_____
_____

Doodle here

Quick list of stuff I've done here :

_____
_____
_____
_____
_____
_____
_____

One major way this place is different from home :

_____
_____
_____
_____

One major way this place is the same as ome :

_____
_____
_____
_____

Place to explore : _____   Date _____

One Moment I want to Remember :

_____
_____
_____
_____
_____
_____
_____
_____
_____

Doodle here

Quick list of stuff I've done here :

_____
_____
_____
_____
_____
_____
_____

One major way this place is different from home :

_____
_____
_____
_____

One major way this place is the same as ome :

_____
_____
_____
_____

Place to explore : _____   Date _____

One Moment I want to Remember :
_____
_____
_____
_____
_____
_____
_____
_____

Doodle here

Quick list of stuff I've done here :
_____
_____
_____
_____
_____
_____
_____

One major way this place is different from home :

_____
_____
_____

One major way this place is the same as ome :

_____
_____
_____

Place to explore : _____ Date _____

One Moment I want to Remember :

_____
_____
_____
_____
_____
_____
_____
_____

Doodle here

Quick list of stuff I've done here :

_____
_____
_____
_____
_____
_____
_____

One major way this place is different from home :

_____
_____
_____
_____

One major way this place is the same as ome :

_____
_____
_____
_____

Place to explore : _____   Date _____

One Moment I want to Remember :

_____
_____
_____
_____
_____
_____
_____
_____

Doodle here

Quick list of stuff I've done here :

_____
_____
_____
_____
_____
_____
_____

One major way this place is different from home :

_____
_____
_____
_____

One major way this place is the same as ome :

_____
_____
_____
_____

Place to explore : _____   Date _____

One Moment I want to Remember :

_____
_____
_____
_____
_____
_____
_____
_____

Doodle here

Quick list of stuff I've done here :

_____
_____
_____
_____
_____
_____
_____

One major way this place is different from home :

_____
_____
_____
_____

One major way this place is the same as ome :

_____
_____
_____
_____

Place to explore : _____   Date _____

One Moment I want to Remember :
_____
_____
_____
_____
_____
_____
_____
_____

Doodle here

Quick list of stuff I've done here :
_____
_____
_____
_____
_____
_____
_____

One major way this place is different from home :

_____
_____
_____

One major way this place is the same as ome :

_____
_____
_____

Place to explore : _____   Date _____

One Moment I want to Remember :

_____
_____
_____
_____
_____
_____
_____
_____
_____

Doodle here

Quick list of stuff I've done here :

_____
_____
_____
_____
_____
_____
_____

One major way this place
is different from home :

_____
_____
_____
_____

One major way this place
is the same as ome :

_____
_____
_____
_____

Place to explore : _____   Date _____

One Moment I want to Remember :

_____
_____
_____
_____
_____
_____
_____
_____
_____

Doodle here

Quick list of stuff I've done here :

_____
_____
_____
_____
_____
_____
_____

One major way this place is different from home :

_____
_____
_____
_____

One major way this place is the same as ome :

_____
_____
_____
_____

Place to explore : _____   Date _____

One Moment I want to Remember :
_____
_____
_____
_____
_____
_____
_____
_____
_____

Doodle here

Quick list of stuff I've done here :
_____
_____
_____
_____
_____
_____
_____

One major way this place is different from home :

_____
_____
_____
_____

One major way this place is the same as ome :

_____
_____
_____
_____

Place to explore : _____   Date _____

One Moment I want to Remember :

_____
_____
_____
_____
_____
_____
_____
_____
_____

Doodle here

Quick list of stuff I've done here :

_____
_____
_____
_____
_____
_____
_____

One major way this place is different from home :

_____
_____
_____

One major way this place is the same as ome :

_____
_____
_____

Place to explore : _____   Date _____

One Moment I want to Remember :

_____
_____
_____
_____
_____
_____
_____
_____

Doodle here

Quick list of stuff I've done here :

_____
_____
_____
_____
_____
_____
_____

One major way this place is different from home :

_____
_____
_____
_____

One major way this place is the same as ome :

_____
_____
_____
_____

Place to explore : _____   Date _____

One Moment I want to Remember :

_____
_____
_____
_____
_____
_____
_____
_____
_____

Doodle here

Quick list of stuff I've done here :

_____
_____
_____
_____
_____
_____
_____

One major way this place
is different from home :

_____
_____
_____
_____

One major way this place
is the same as ome :

_____
_____
_____
_____

Place to explore : _____   Date _____

One Moment I want to Remember :

_____
_____
_____
_____
_____
_____
_____
_____
_____

Doodle here

Quick list of stuff I've done here :

_____
_____
_____
_____
_____
_____
_____

One major way this place is different from home :

_____
_____
_____
_____

One major way this place is the same as ome :

_____
_____
_____
_____

Place to explore : _____   Date _____

One Moment I want to Remember :
_____
_____
_____
_____
_____
_____
_____
_____
_____

Doodle here

Quick list of stuff I've done here :
_____
_____
_____
_____
_____
_____
_____

One major way this place
is different from home :

One major way this place
is the same as ome :

_____   _____
_____   _____
_____   _____
_____   _____

Place to explore : _____   Date _____

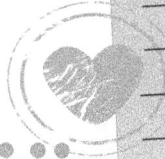

One Moment I want to Remember :

_____
_____
_____
_____
_____
_____
_____
_____

Doodle here

Quick list of stuff I've done here :

_____
_____
_____
_____
_____
_____
_____

One major way this place is different from home :

_____
_____
_____
_____

One major way this place is the same as ome :

_____
_____
_____
_____

Place to explore : _____   Date _____

One Moment I want to Remember :

_____
_____
_____
_____
_____
_____
_____
_____

Doodle here

Quick list of stuff I've done here :

_____
_____
_____
_____
_____
_____

One major way this place is different from home :

_____
_____
_____

One major way this place is the same as ome :

_____
_____
_____

Place to explore : _____   Date _____

One Moment I want to Remember :

_____
_____
_____
_____
_____
_____
_____
_____
_____

Doodle here

Quick list of stuff I've done here :

_____
_____
_____
_____
_____
_____
_____

One major way this place is different from home :

_____
_____
_____
_____

One major way this place is the same as ome :

_____
_____
_____
_____

Place to explore : _____   Date _____

One Moment I want to Remember :

_____

_____

_____

_____

_____

_____

_____

_____

_____

Doodle here

Quick list of stuff I've done here :

_____

_____

_____

_____

_____

_____

One major way this place is different from home :

_____

_____

_____

_____

One major way this place is the same as ome :

_____

_____

_____

_____

Place to explore : _____   Date _____

One Moment I want to Remember :

_____
_____
_____
_____
_____
_____
_____
_____
_____

Doodle here

Quick list of stuff I've done here :

_____
_____
_____
_____
_____
_____
_____

One major way this place is different from home :

_____
_____
_____
_____

One major way this place is the same as ome :

_____
_____
_____
_____

Place to explore : _____   Date _____

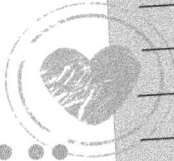

One Moment I want to Remember :

_____
_____
_____
_____
_____
_____
_____
_____
_____

Doodle here

Quick list of stuff I've done here :

_____
_____
_____
_____
_____
_____
_____

One major way this place is different from home :

_____
_____
_____
_____

One major way this place is the same as ome :

_____
_____
_____
_____

Place to explore : _____   Date _____

One Moment I want to Remember :

_____
_____
_____
_____
_____
_____
_____
_____

Doodle here

Quick list of stuff I've done here :

_____
_____
_____
_____
_____
_____
_____

One major way this place is different from home :

_____
_____
_____
_____

One major way this place is the same as ome :

_____
_____
_____
_____

Place to explore : _____   Date _____

One Moment I want to Remember :
_____
_____
_____
_____
_____
_____
_____
_____
_____

Doodle here

Quick list of stuff I've done here :
_____
_____
_____
_____
_____
_____
_____

One major way this place is different from home :

_____
_____
_____
_____

One major way this place is the same as ome :

_____
_____
_____
_____

Place to explore : _____   Date _____

One Moment I want to Remember :

_____
_____
_____
_____
_____
_____
_____
_____
_____

Doodle here

Quick list of stuff I've done here :

_____
_____
_____
_____
_____
_____
_____

One major way this place is different from home :

_____
_____
_____
_____

One major way this place is the same as ome :

_____
_____
_____
_____

Place to explore : _____   Date _____

One Moment I want to Remember :
_____
_____
_____
_____
_____
_____
_____
_____
_____

Doodle here

Quick list of stuff I've done here :
_____
_____
_____
_____
_____
_____
_____

One major way this place is different from home :

_____
_____
_____
_____

One major way this place is the same as ome :

_____
_____
_____
_____

Place to explore : _____   Date _____

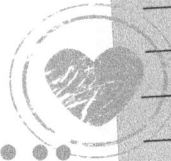

One Moment I want to Remember :

_____
_____
_____
_____
_____
_____
_____
_____
_____
_____

Doodle here

Quick list of stuff I've done here :

_____
_____
_____
_____
_____
_____
_____

One major way this place is different from home :

_____
_____
_____
_____

One major way this place is the same as ome :

_____
_____
_____
_____

Place to explore : _____   Date _____

One Moment I want to Remember :
_____
_____
_____
_____
_____
_____
_____
_____
_____

Doodle here

Quick list of stuff I've done here :
_____
_____
_____
_____
_____
_____
_____

One major way this place is different from home :

_____
_____
_____
_____

One major way this place is the same as ome :

_____
_____
_____
_____

Place to explore : _____   Date _____

One Moment I want to Remember :

_____
_____
_____
_____
_____
_____
_____
_____

Doodle here

Quick list of stuff I've done here :

_____
_____
_____
_____
_____
_____
_____

One major way this place   One major way this place
is different from home :   is the same as ome :

_____   _____
_____   _____
_____   _____
_____   _____

Place to explore : _____   Date _____

One Moment I want to Remember :

_____
_____
_____
_____
_____
_____
_____
_____
_____

Doodle here

Quick list of stuff I've done here :

_____
_____
_____
_____
_____
_____
_____

One major way this place is different from home :

_____
_____
_____
_____

One major way this place is the same as ome :

_____
_____
_____
_____

Place to explore : _____   Date _____

One Moment I want to Remember :

_____
_____
_____
_____
_____
_____
_____
_____

Doodle here

Quick list of stuff I've done here :

_____
_____
_____
_____
_____
_____
_____

One major way this place is different from home :

_____
_____
_____
_____

One major way this place is the same as ome :

_____
_____
_____
_____

Place to explore : _____   Date _____

One Moment I want to Remember :

_____
_____
_____
_____
_____
_____
_____
_____
_____
_____

Doodle here

Quick list of stuff I've done here :

_____
_____
_____
_____
_____
_____
_____

One major way this place is different from home :

_____
_____
_____
_____

One major way this place is the same as ome :

_____
_____
_____
_____

Place to explore : _____   Date _____

One Moment I want to Remember :

_____
_____
_____
_____
_____
_____
_____
_____
_____

Doodle here

Quick list of stuff I've done here :

_____
_____
_____
_____
_____
_____
_____

One major way this place is different from home :

_____
_____
_____
_____

One major way this place is the same as ome :

_____
_____
_____
_____

Place to explore : _____ Date _____

One Moment I want to Remember :
_____
_____
_____
_____
_____
_____
_____
_____
_____

Doodle here

Quick list of stuff I've done here :
_____
_____
_____
_____
_____
_____
_____

One major way this place is different from home :

_____
_____
_____
_____

One major way this place is the same as ome :

_____
_____
_____
_____

Place to explore : _____   Date _____

One Moment I want to Remember :

_____
_____
_____
_____
_____
_____
_____
_____
_____

Doodle here

Quick list of stuff I've done here :

_____
_____
_____
_____
_____
_____
_____

One major way this place is different from home :

_____
_____
_____
_____

One major way this place is the same as ome :

_____
_____
_____
_____

Place to explore : _____   Date _____

One Moment I want to Remember :

_____
_____
_____
_____
_____
_____
_____
_____

Doodle here

Quick list of stuff I've done here :

_____
_____
_____
_____
_____
_____
_____

One major way this place is different from home :

_____
_____
_____

One major way this place is the same as ome :

_____
_____
_____

Place to explore : _____   Date _____

One Moment I want to Remember :

_____
_____
_____
_____
_____
_____
_____
_____

Doodle here

Quick list of stuff I've done here :

_____
_____
_____
_____
_____
_____
_____

One major way this place is different from home :

_____
_____
_____
_____

One major way this place is the same as ome :

_____
_____
_____
_____

Place to explore : _____   Date _____

One Moment I want to Remember :
_____
_____
_____
_____
_____
_____
_____
_____

Doodle here

Quick list of stuff I've done here :
_____
_____
_____
_____
_____
_____
_____

One major way this place is different from home :

_____
_____
_____
_____

One major way this place is the same as ome :

_____
_____
_____
_____

Place to explore : _____   Date _____

One Moment I want to Remember :

_____
_____
_____
_____
_____
_____
_____
_____
_____

Doodle here

Quick list of stuff I've done here :

_____
_____
_____
_____
_____
_____
_____

One major way this place is different from home :

_____
_____
_____
_____

One major way this place is the same as ome :

_____
_____
_____
_____

Place to explore : _____   Date _____

One Moment I want to Remember :

_____
_____
_____
_____
_____
_____
_____
_____

Doodle here

Quick list of stuff I've done here :

_____
_____
_____
_____
_____
_____
_____

One major way this place is different from home :

_____
_____
_____
_____

One major way this place is the same as ome :

_____
_____
_____
_____

Place to explore : _____   Date _____

One Moment I want to Remember :

_____
_____
_____
_____
_____
_____
_____
_____

Doodle here

Quick list of stuff I've done here :

_____
_____
_____
_____
_____
_____
_____

One major way this place is different from home :

_____
_____
_____
_____

One major way this place is the same as ome :

_____
_____
_____
_____

Place to explore : _____   Date _____

One Moment I want to Remember :

_____
_____
_____
_____
_____
_____
_____
_____
_____

Doodle here

Quick list of stuff I've done here :

_____
_____
_____
_____
_____
_____
_____

One major way this place is different from home :

_____
_____
_____
_____

One major way this place is the same as ome :

_____
_____
_____
_____

Place to explore : _____   Date _____

One Moment I want to Remember :

_____
_____
_____
_____
_____
_____
_____
_____

Doodle here

Quick list of stuff I've done here :

_____
_____
_____
_____
_____
_____
_____

One major way this place is different from home :

_____
_____
_____
_____

One major way this place is the same as ome :

_____
_____
_____
_____

Place to explore : _____   Date _____

One Moment I want to Remember :

_____
_____
_____
_____
_____
_____
_____
_____
_____

Doodle here

Quick list of stuff I've done here :

_____
_____
_____
_____
_____
_____
_____

One major way this place is different from home :

_____
_____
_____
_____

One major way this place is the same as ome :

_____
_____
_____
_____

Place to explore : _____   Date _____

One Moment I want to Remember :

_____
_____
_____
_____
_____
_____
_____
_____
_____

Doodle here

Quick list of stuff I've done here :

_____
_____
_____
_____
_____
_____
_____

One major way this place
is different from home :

_____
_____
_____
_____

One major way this place
is the same as ome :

_____
_____
_____
_____

Place to explore : _____   Date _____

One Moment I want to Remember :

_____
_____
_____
_____
_____
_____
_____
_____
_____

Doodle here

Quick list of stuff I've done here :

_____
_____
_____
_____
_____
_____
_____

One major way this place is different from home :

_____
_____
_____
_____

One major way this place is the same as ome :

_____
_____
_____
_____

Place to explore : _____   Date _____

One Moment I want to Remember :

_____

_____

_____

_____

_____

_____

_____

_____

Doodle here

Quick list of stuff I've done here :

_____

_____

_____

_____

_____

_____

_____

One major way this place is different from home :

_____

_____

_____

_____

One major way this place is the same as ome :

_____

_____

_____

_____

Place to explore : _____   Date _____

One Moment I want to Remember :
_____
_____
_____
_____
_____
_____
_____
_____
_____
_____

Doodle here

Quick list of stuff I've done here :
_____
_____
_____
_____
_____
_____
_____

One major way this place is different from home :

_____
_____
_____

One major way this place is the same as ome :

_____
_____
_____

Place to explore : _____   Date _____

One Moment I want to Remember :
_____
_____
_____
_____
_____
_____
_____
_____

Doodle here

Quick list of stuff I've done here :
_____
_____
_____
_____
_____
_____
_____

One major way this place is different from home :

_____
_____
_____
_____

One major way this place is the same as ome :

_____
_____
_____
_____

Place to explore : _____ Date _____

One Moment I want to Remember :
_____
_____
_____
_____
_____
_____
_____
_____

Doodle here

Quick list of stuff I've done here :
_____
_____
_____
_____
_____
_____
_____

One major way this place is different from home :

One major way this place is the same as ome :

_____   _____
_____   _____
_____   _____
_____   _____

Place to explore : _____   Date _____

One Moment I want to Remember :

_____
_____
_____
_____
_____
_____
_____
_____
_____

Doodle here

Quick list of stuff I've done here :

_____
_____
_____
_____
_____
_____
_____

One major way this place is different from home :

_____
_____
_____
_____

One major way this place is the same as ome :

_____
_____
_____
_____

Place to explore : _____   Date _____

One Moment I want to Remember :

_____
_____
_____
_____
_____
_____
_____
_____

Doodle here

Quick list of stuff I've done here :

_____
_____
_____
_____
_____
_____
_____

One major way this place is different from home :

_____
_____
_____
_____

One major way this place is the same as ome :

_____
_____
_____
_____

Place to explore : _____ Date _____

One Moment I want to Remember :

_____
_____
_____
_____
_____
_____
_____
_____
_____

Doodle here

Quick list of stuff I've done here :

_____
_____
_____
_____
_____
_____
_____

One major way this place is different from home :

_____
_____
_____
_____

One major way this place is the same as ome :

_____
_____
_____
_____

Place to explore : _____   Date _____

One Moment I want to Remember :

_____
_____
_____
_____
_____
_____
_____
_____
_____

Doodle here

Quick list of stuff I've done here :

_____
_____
_____
_____
_____
_____
_____

One major way this place is different from home :

_____
_____
_____
_____

One major way this place is the same as ome :

_____
_____
_____
_____

Place to explore : _____   Date _____

One Moment I want to Remember :

_____
_____
_____
_____
_____
_____
_____
_____
_____
_____

Doodle here

Quick list of stuff I've done here :
_____
_____
_____
_____
_____
_____
_____

One major way this place   One major way this place
is different from home :   is the same as ome :

_____   _____
_____   _____
_____   _____
_____   _____

Place to explore : _____   Date _____

One Moment I want to Remember :

_____
_____
_____
_____
_____
_____
_____
_____
_____

Doodle here

Quick list of stuff I've done here :

_____
_____
_____
_____
_____
_____
_____

One major way this place is different from home :

_____
_____
_____

One major way this place is the same as ome :

_____
_____
_____

Place to explore : _____   Date _____

One Moment I want to Remember :
_____
_____
_____
_____
_____
_____
_____
_____
_____

Doodle here

Quick list of stuff I've done here :
_____
_____
_____
_____
_____
_____
_____

One major way this place is different from home :

_____

_____

_____

_____

One major way this place is the same as ome :

_____

_____

_____

_____

Place to explore : _____   Date _____

One Moment I want to Remember :

_____
_____
_____
_____
_____
_____
_____
_____
_____

Doodle here

Quick list of stuff I've done here :

_____
_____
_____
_____
_____
_____
_____

One major way this place is different from home :

_____
_____
_____
_____

One major way this place is the same as ome :

_____
_____
_____
_____

Place to explore : _____   Date _____

One Moment I want to Remember :
_____
_____
_____
_____
_____
_____
_____
_____
_____

Doodle here

Quick list of stuff I've done here :
_____
_____
_____
_____
_____
_____
_____

One major way this place is different from home :

_____
_____
_____
_____

One major way this place is the same as ome :

_____
_____
_____
_____

Place to explore : _____ Date _____

One Moment I want to Remember :

_____

_____

_____

_____

_____

_____

_____

_____

Doodle here

Quick list of stuff I've done here :

_____

_____

_____

_____

_____

_____

_____

One major way this place is different from home :

_____

_____

_____

One major way this place is the same as ome :

_____

_____

_____

Place to explore : _____   Date _____

One Moment I want to Remember :
_____
_____
_____
_____
_____
_____
_____
_____

Doodle here

Quick list of stuff I've done here :
_____
_____
_____
_____
_____
_____
_____

One major way this place is different from home :

_____
_____
_____
_____

One major way this place is the same as ome :

_____
_____
_____
_____

Place to explore : _____   Date _____

One Moment I want to Remember :

_____
_____
_____
_____
_____
_____
_____
_____

Doodle here

Quick list of stuff I've done here :

_____
_____
_____
_____
_____
_____
_____

One major way this place is different from home :

_____
_____
_____
_____

One major way this place is the same as ome :

_____
_____
_____
_____

Place to explore : _____   Date _____

One Moment I want to Remember :

_____
_____
_____
_____
_____
_____
_____
_____
_____

Doodle here

Quick list of stuff I've done here :

_____
_____
_____
_____
_____
_____
_____

One major way this place is different from home :

_____
_____
_____
_____

One major way this place is the same as ome :

_____
_____
_____
_____

Place to explore : _____ Date _____

One Moment I want to Remember :

_____
_____
_____
_____
_____
_____
_____
_____

Doodle here

Quick list of stuff I've done here :

_____
_____
_____
_____
_____
_____
_____

One major way this place is different from home :

_____
_____
_____
_____

One major way this place is the same as ome :

_____
_____
_____
_____

Place to explore : _____   Date _____

One Moment I want to Remember :

_____
_____
_____
_____
_____
_____
_____

Doodle here

Quick list of stuff I've done here :

_____
_____
_____
_____
_____
_____
_____

One major way this place is different from home :

_____
_____
_____
_____

One major way this place is the same as ome :

_____
_____
_____
_____

Place to explore : _____   Date _____

One Moment I want to Remember :

_____
_____
_____
_____
_____
_____
_____
_____

Doodle here

Quick list of stuff I've done here :

_____
_____
_____
_____
_____
_____
_____

One major way this place is different from home :

_____
_____
_____
_____

One major way this place is the same as ome :

_____
_____
_____
_____

Place to explore : _____ Date _____

One Moment I want to Remember :

_____
_____
_____
_____
_____
_____
_____
_____
_____
_____

Doodle here

Quick list of stuff I've done here :

_____
_____
_____
_____
_____
_____
_____

One major way this place is different from home :

_____
_____
_____
_____

One major way this place is the same as ome :

_____
_____
_____
_____

Place to explore : _____   Date _____

One Moment I want to Remember :
_____
_____
_____
_____
_____
_____
_____
_____
_____
_____

Doodle here

Quick list of stuff I've done here :
_____
_____
_____
_____
_____
_____
_____

One major way this place
is different from home :

One major way this place
is the same as ome :

_____   _____
_____   _____
_____   _____
_____   _____

Place to explore : _____   Date _____

One Moment I want to Remember :
_____
_____
_____
_____
_____
_____
_____
_____

Doodle here

Quick list of stuff I've done here :
_____
_____
_____
_____
_____
_____
_____

One major way this place is different from home :

_____
_____
_____
_____

One major way this place is the same as ome :

_____
_____
_____
_____

Place to explore : _____   Date _____

One Moment I want to Remember :
_____
_____
_____
_____
_____
_____
_____
_____
_____
_____

Doodle here

Quick list of stuff I've done here :
_____
_____
_____
_____
_____
_____
_____

One major way this place is different from home :

_____
_____
_____

One major way this place is the same as ome :

_____
_____
_____

Place to explore : _____   Date _____

One Moment I want to Remember :
_____
_____
_____
_____
_____
_____
_____
_____
_____

Doodle here

Quick list of stuff I've done here :
_____
_____
_____
_____
_____
_____
_____

One major way this place is different from home :

_____
_____
_____
_____

One major way this place is the same as ome :

_____
_____
_____
_____

Place to explore : _____   Date _____

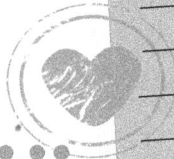

One Moment I want to Remember :

_____
_____
_____
_____
_____
_____
_____
_____
_____
_____

Doodle here

Quick list of stuff I've done here :

_____
_____
_____
_____
_____
_____
_____

One major way this place
is different from home :

_____
_____
_____
_____

One major way this place
is the same as ome :

_____
_____
_____
_____

Place to explore : _____   Date _____

One Moment I want to Remember :
_____
_____
_____
_____
_____
_____
_____
_____

Doodle here

Quick list of stuff I've done here :
_____
_____
_____
_____
_____
_____
_____

One major way this place is different from home :

_____
_____
_____
_____

One major way this place is the same as ome :

_____
_____
_____
_____

Place to explore : _____   Date _____

One Moment I want to Remember :
_____
_____
_____
_____
_____
_____
_____
_____
_____

Doodle here

Quick list of stuff I've done here :
_____
_____
_____
_____
_____
_____
_____

One major way this place is different from home :

_____
_____
_____
_____

One major way this place is the same as ome :

_____
_____
_____
_____

Place to explore : _____   Date _____

One Moment I want to Remember :

_____

_____

_____

_____

_____

_____

_____

_____

Doodle here

Quick list of stuff I've done here :

_____

_____

_____

_____

_____

_____

_____

One major way this place is different from home :

_____

_____

_____

One major way this place is the same as ome :

_____

_____

_____

Place to explore : _____   Date _____

One Moment I want to Remember :
_____
_____
_____
_____
_____
_____
_____
_____
_____
_____

Doodle here

Quick list of stuff I've done here :
_____
_____
_____
_____
_____
_____
_____
_____

One major way this place is different from home :
_____
_____
_____
_____

One major way this place is the same as ome :
_____
_____
_____
_____

Place to explore : _____   Date _____

One Moment I want to Remember :

_____
_____
_____
_____
_____
_____
_____
_____

Doodle here

Quick list of stuff I've done here :

_____
_____
_____
_____
_____
_____
_____

One major way this place is different from home :

_____
_____
_____
_____

One major way this place is the same as ome :

_____
_____
_____
_____

Place to explore : _____   Date _____

One Moment I want to Remember :

_____
_____
_____
_____
_____
_____
_____
_____

Doodle here

Quick list of stuff I've done here :

_____
_____
_____
_____
_____
_____
_____

One major way this place is different from home :

_____
_____
_____
_____

One major way this place is the same as ome :

_____
_____
_____
_____

Place to explore : _____   Date _____

One Moment I want to Remember :
_____
_____
_____
_____
_____
_____
_____
_____
_____

Doodle here

Quick list of stuff I've done here :
_____
_____
_____
_____
_____
_____
_____

One major way this place is different from home :

_____
_____
_____
_____

One major way this place is the same as ome :

_____
_____
_____
_____

Place to explore : _____   Date _____

One Moment I want to Remember :

_____
_____
_____
_____
_____
_____
_____
_____
_____

Doodle here

Quick list of stuff I've done here :

_____
_____
_____
_____
_____
_____
_____
_____

One major way this place is different from home :

_____
_____
_____
_____

One major way this place is the same as ome :

_____
_____
_____
_____

Place to explore : _____   Date _____

One Moment I want to Remember :

_____

_____

_____

_____

_____

_____

_____

_____

Doodle here

Quick list of stuff I've done here :

_____

_____

_____

_____

_____

_____

_____

One major way this place
is different from home :

_____

_____

_____

_____

One major way this place
is the same as ome :

_____

_____

_____

_____

Place to explore : _____   Date _____

One Moment I want to Remember :
_____
_____
_____
_____
_____
_____
_____
_____

Doodle here

Quick list of stuff I've done here :
_____
_____
_____
_____
_____
_____
_____

One major way this place is different from home :

One major way this place is the same as ome :

_____   _____
_____   _____
_____   _____

Place to explore : _____   Date _____

One Moment I want to Remember :

_____
_____
_____
_____
_____
_____
_____
_____
_____

Doodle here

Quick list of stuff I've done here :

_____
_____
_____
_____
_____
_____
_____

One major way this place is different from home :

_____
_____
_____
_____

One major way this place is the same as ome :

_____
_____
_____
_____

Place to explore : _____ Date _____

One Moment I want to Remember :

_____
_____
_____
_____
_____
_____
_____
_____
_____

Doodle here

Quick list of stuff I've done here :

_____
_____
_____
_____
_____
_____
_____

One major way this place is different from home :

_____
_____
_____
_____

One major way this place is the same as ome :

_____
_____
_____
_____

Place to explore : _____   Date _____

One Moment I want to Remember :

_____
_____
_____
_____
_____
_____
_____
_____

Doodle here

Quick list of stuff I've done here :

_____
_____
_____
_____
_____
_____
_____

One major way this place is different from home :

_____
_____
_____
_____

One major way this place is the same as ome :

_____
_____
_____
_____

Place to explore : _____   Date _____

One Moment I want to Remember :

_____
_____
_____
_____
_____
_____
_____
_____
_____

Doodle here

Quick list of stuff I've done here :

_____
_____
_____
_____
_____
_____
_____

One major way this place is different from home :

_____
_____
_____
_____

One major way this place is the same as ome :

_____
_____
_____
_____

Place to explore : _____   Date _____

One Moment I want to Remember :

_____
_____
_____
_____
_____
_____
_____
_____
_____

Doodle here

Quick list of stuff I've done here :

_____
_____
_____
_____
_____
_____
_____

One major way this place is different from home :

_____
_____
_____
_____

One major way this place is the same as ome :

_____
_____
_____
_____

Place to explore : _____ Date _____

One Moment I want to Remember :
_____
_____
_____
_____
_____
_____
_____
_____
_____

Doodle here

Quick list of stuff I've done here :
_____
_____
_____
_____
_____
_____
_____

One major way this place is different from home :
_____
_____
_____
_____

One major way this place is the same as ome :
_____
_____
_____
_____

Place to explore : _____ Date _____

One Moment I want to Remember :

_____
_____
_____
_____
_____
_____
_____
_____

Doodle here

Quick list of stuff I've done here :

_____
_____
_____
_____
_____
_____
_____

One major way this place is different from home :

_____
_____
_____
_____

One major way this place is the same as ome :

_____
_____
_____
_____

Place to explore : _____   Date _____

One Moment I want to Remember :

_____
_____
_____
_____
_____
_____
_____
_____

Doodle here

Quick list of stuff I've done here :
_____
_____
_____
_____
_____
_____
_____

One major way this place is different from home :

_____
_____
_____
_____

One major way this place is the same as ome :

_____
_____
_____
_____

Place to explore : _____   Date _____

One Moment I want to Remember :

_____
_____
_____
_____
_____
_____
_____
_____

Doodle here

Quick list of stuff I've done here :

_____
_____
_____
_____
_____
_____
_____

One major way this place is different from home :

_____
_____
_____
_____

One major way this place is the same as ome :

_____
_____
_____
_____

Place to explore : _____   Date _____

One Moment I want to Remember :
_____
_____
_____
_____
_____
_____
_____
_____
_____

Doodle here

Quick list of stuff I've done here :
_____
_____
_____
_____
_____
_____
_____

One major way this place is different from home :

_____
_____
_____
_____

One major way this place is the same as ome :

_____
_____
_____
_____

www.ingramcontent.com/pod-product-compliance
Lightning Source LLC
Chambersburg PA
CBHW081333090426
42737CB00017B/3120